Big
and small

First published in Great Britain 1989
by Octopus Publishing Group for
The Parent and Child Programme
Published 1997 by Mammoth
an imprint of Reed International Books Limited
Michelin House, 81 Fulham Road, London, SW3 6RB
and Auckland, Melbourne, Singapore and Toronto

10 9 8 7 6 5 4 3 2 1

Copyright © Reed International Books Limited 1989

0 7497 3016 1

A CIP catalogue record for this title
is available from the British Library

Produced by Mandarin Offset Ltd
Printed and bound in Hong Kong

Big
and small

Written and devised by
David Bennett

Illustrated by
Louise Voce

I am teeny-tiny,
I creep and I crawl.
I'm sure that I am
The smallest of all.

Who am I?

I am bigger than her,
But still rather small.
I can run very fast,
Although I'm not tall.

Who am I?

I am bigger than him,
But still small and sweet.
I go quack, quack, quack
And not tweet, tweet, tweet.

Who am I?

I am bigger than her,
I can leap, jump and run
And chasing young birds
Is my best kind of fun.

Who am I?

I am bigger than him,
I bark and I play.
With one look at me,
The cat runs away.

Who am I?

I am bigger than her
And I eat, eat, eat.
I am fat, pink and round,
With stubby little feet.

Who am I?

I am bigger than him,
I grunt and I growl.
You had better watch out
When I'm on the prowl.

Who am I?

I am bigger than her,
So just listen to me.
I splash in the mud,
Till I'm ready for tea.

Who am I?

I am bigger than him,
Much bigger by far.
My ears and long nose
Make me the star.

Who am I?

Who is big
And who is small?
Who is the biggest
Of us all?